LAURA CERWINSKE

TROPICAL DECO

THE ARCHITECTURE AND DESIGN
OF OLD MIAMI BEACH

photography by David Kaminsky

RIZZOLI

cover and graphics by Woody Vondracek

Text © 1981 by Laura Cerwinske
Photographs © 1981 by David Kaminsky
Published in the United States of America in 1981 by
Rizzoli International Publications, Inc.
300 Park Avenue South, New York, NY 10010

ISBN: 0-8478-0345-7   LC: 80-51596
Printed in Japan

For Evie and Bob, my gift of thanks for your
lifetime of gifts of love.

ACKNOWLEDGEMENTS

My love and thanks always to Harry Warren, who not only taught me how to write, but who also shows me continually the meaning of dedication.

Several of the photographs appearing in this book were originally taken in conjunction with a project for the Miami Design Preservation League, funded by a grant from the National Endowment for the Arts in Washington, D.C. a federal agency.

Note: The Miami Beach Art Deco District is located officially (according to the National Register of Historic Places) between Fifth Street to the south and 23rd Street to the north; and from Ocean Drive on the east to Lenox Court on the west. Many wonderful examples of Art Deco architecture also lie outside the District. When illustrated in this book, they are noted with an asterisk.

photograph of Cinema Theatre (p. 107) by Les Rachline

CONTENTS

PREFACE

Born out of fantasy and speculation, designed for fun and profit, Miami Beach, from its inception, has been a city of mythical composition. Today, its famed Art Deco District succeeds as one of America's favorite fictions. As a scenic backdrop for tv series and fashion spreads, it is a dream location; as an investment opportunity, it is a developers' playground. Yet, it is also a crime-ridden oceanfront neighborhood, a faded resort in transition, a municipality whose byzantine city government, for years, has allowed it to flounder in a sea of physical ruin while believers in its once and future charm propelled its magical image around the world.

Having struggled along for the last ten years to recreate itself from its own forgotten glamour, the Art Deco District is now plunging into its newest metamorphosis. Since 1985, entrepreneurs, developers, restaurateurs, club owners and artists have been putting down stakes in the area in a big way. This activity is the outgrowth of efforts begun more than ten years ago when a group called the Miami Design Preservation League first organized to halt the city's deterioration by bringing attention to the significance of its architecture. As a result, one square mile, containing over 400 buildings in the Art Deco style and representing the largest community of Deco buildings in the world, was designated a Historic District by the National Register of Historic Places in 1979.

The Historic designation was significant not only for Miami Beach, but also, more generally, as an expression of changing attitudes toward "history." It reflected a new willingness to alter our perceptions of the immediate past and to examine more closely the contexts of our lives. Because of the physical disposability of much of present day society, we are no longer shocked when multi-storied, multi-million dollar structures deteriorate within a few years of being built. Historically, however, public architecture was designed for perpetuity. In spiritually directed cultures, its aim, at least metaphorically, was toward eternity.

Modern architecture's rebellion against traditional ideologies was accompanied by technological evolution and the desire of modern architects for a new structural language. While groping to express the demands and radically new perspectives of twentieth century culture, modern architects refracted traditional vision and reshaped architecture's role. Heavy stone buttressing was no longer needed to support monumental churches and their monumental doctrines. Steel framing and reinforced concrete gave buildings self-sufficient strength allowing thin skins of glass to envelop skyscrapers of inconceivable heights and affording their occupants, for the first time in history, unrestricted visibility. In the process, however, modern architecture erased the traditional frames (such as the window and the articulated door) by which we had heretofore understood our relation to the landscape and to the building itself and replaced them with cerebral, abstract and, ultimately, disorienting compositions.

Despite the sense of adventure that characterized the early mood of Modernism, its result was alienating and difficult to execute well (Miesian design is too precisely detailed and too expensive for most architects to carry out properly). That technology now has made it possible for buildings to go up almost as fast as they can be torn down makes it all the more ironic to contemplate how, in the rush to become "modern," contemporary architecture planted the seeds of its own demise within its own conception.

Though Miami Beach's Art Deco architecture was built predominantly during the 1930s, when Modernist hopes were at their peak, it nonetheless decked itself out with decorative embellishments and narrative allusions. It adapted Modernist streamlining to make its buildings look like oceanliners and turned precision into fantasy.

Inventiveness and bravado have always made for much of Miami Beach's uniqueness, and, in fact, its humanizing quirks and commentaries account for much of the Art Deco District's present allure. But despite the heartening interest in the neighborhood's preservation, the nature of its reuse is, perhaps, the most critical question in terms of its ultimate survival. Though preserving its scale and character are essential, its real opportunities lie in reinvention. New materials and updated design concepts offer to enrich the District more than literal re-creation. Reinterpret it as an urban neighborhood (rather than repeating its now limited resort potential), and the city will gain activity, diversity and new life.

Actually, in one regard, the Deco buildings already have been graphically reinterpreted and are ready to return to a look closer to their original. Five years ago interior designer Leonard Horowitz, who grew up on Miami Beach, created a palette of tropical pastels, replacing the dark, dreary, inappropriate browns and beiges they had been painted during the 1970s. As the pinks and turquoises and lavenders spread from building to building and block to block, the radically bright and photogenic new look generated public attention that years of political rallying could never achieve. But, today, the value of the confectionary tones has run its course, and their effect has become trendy and tiresome, giving the District a sort of decorator look.

Thus, ironically, what serves the Deco buildings best is what served them first: Modernist white facades with seafoam green, powder blue and salmon pink trims.

Clean, classic, and full of light, the modest white hotels and apartments reveled in their own dignity and crispness.

One final contradiction in the curious history of the Art Deco District concerns the political attitude of the City of Miami Beach toward the neighborhood. Despite the national Historic Designation almost ten years ago, the buildings have remained virtually unprotected from demolition and scarcely guided redevelopment with no local legislation to protect them. In fact, the one factor that has served most to save them has been the area's depressed economy.

The City, however, finally acknowledged a value in preserving its Art Deco architecture in 1986 by creating a local preservation district (one quarter the size of the national designation) covering Collins Avenue and Ocean Drive. While Deco buildings still can be torn down, the new legislation provides a six-month delay from the time a property owner requests demolition, allowing time for another investor to step in or for the owner to be convinced by the city administration of the benefits of rehabilitation.

The Miami Beach Art Deco Distrct epitomizes pioneering hope equally as it illustrates cultural despair. Somewhere in the midst of the chic and trendy aspirations of most of its current developers and the abandoned haze of its outcast elderly and Latin population lies a neighborhood waiting for youth, activity and originality to reenergize it. It does not need to become more fancy, but more fun. Though it has already emerged as Miami's most hip after-hours scene, the trick in accomplishing its real success is to turn it from a late night hot spot into a lively, safe and amusing daytime community too. With one of the cleanest and most uncrowded public beaches in the country, cruise ships hovering on its horizon and Fragonard clouds animating its tropically blue sky, how hard can that really be?

INTRODUCTION

THE EVOLUTION OF "DECO"

The origin of the term "Art Deco" as we know it today has, in fact, two sources. The first is derived from the synthesis of numerous exotic and dynamic influences which culminated in an exclusive fashion of high taste in Europe—primarily Paris—during the first two decades of the twentieth century. This Art Deco style was nurtured by the drama and fantastic design of Diaghilev's "Ballet Russe," by the exoticism of African art and the refinement of Oriental art, and by a love for sensuous textures and exquisitely applied ornament. It was a style of rich surfaces, and it luxuriated in the use of rare and expensive materials—ivory, ebony, mother-of-pearl, semi-precious stones, unusual woods, crystal and marble. Art Deco capitalized on images of mystical and romantic animals—peacocks, greyhounds, and borzois—and it represented nature in its fluidity, with an abundance of fountains, gladiolas, shells, and other organic motifs.

Concurrent with the development of Art Deco in Europe, and also influential upon it, were the works of other creative forces: the Futurists in Italy who were enamored with speed and slashed away at the old space-time restrictions of the picture plane; the Cubists, who energized that plane with suggestions of a new dimension and geometry; and the artists Dali and Cocteau, who thwarted minds with new surrealistic images. The style was also influenced by the esoteric cultures of the Moors, Aztecs, Mayas, and Assyrians, and by the mysteriousness of the pre-Raphaelites.

The second source for "Art Deco" came from the assimilation of this rich European style into the American culture of the 1920s and 30s. World War I was instrumental in importing the most contemporary European cultural developments to the American public. It was also responsible for the relaxation of numerous social traditions and inhibitions which changed Western society. Moreover, expanded communications in the forms of radio, telephone, magazines and movies; broadened travel via the automobile, ocean liner, locomotive and airplane; and the gearing up of mass production in national industry all heralded a new American consciousness.

As the Art Deco style began to permeate American design, sleek and shiny cars and trains became favorite images. Lightning-bolt zig-zags added a forceful angularity. And the depiction of human figures evolved from the earlier languid Art Nouveau poses to more sinewy, sultry, and stylized postures. The discovery in Egypt of King Tutankhamen's tomb in 1921 had a strong effect on both the European and American adaptations of the Deco style as the color, geometry, and unfathomable richness of ancient Egyptian art was eagerly absorbed.

In 1925 the first international exhibition organized solely for the applied arts in over 100 years took place in Paris. It included displays of artistic work in glass, bookbinding, ceramics, textiles, wrought iron, and covered every branch of the decorative arts from complete interiors to children's toys. This Design Fair, in which the development of this promiscuous and eclectic style culminated, was called the "Exposition Internationale des Arts Decoratifs et Industriels Modernes," and its abbreviated title, "Arts Deco," gave the style its official name, later to be known as "Art Deco." It also inadvertantly brought about a reorientation of American design. Upon being invited to exhibit at the Paris Exposition, American designers realized they had nothing to submit that was representative of the U.S. character. American arts were still highly derivative, fixed upon such antique and period styles as American Colonial, Spanish and Italian Renaissance, Tudor and eighteenth century French and English. As the American decorator Paul Frankl explained, "... we found we had no decorative art. Not only was there a sad lack of any achievement that could be exhibited, but we discovered that there was not even a serious movement in this direction and that the general public was quite unconscious of the fact that modern art extended into the field of business and industry."[2]

This was a startling recognition, and it initiated an important period of self examination. For us today—after five decades of prolific American cultural ingenuity and its global impact —it is hard to imagine that in the 1920s America acknowledged no wholly American fine art form to exist. Though the U.S. by no means closed herself off from external influences in this period, she did turn inward to seek the primary resources for her artistic inspiration.

This introspection was unprecedented and produced expressions of amazing power and scope from which evolved many of the classic designs we consistently employ today. These cultural explorations integrated a phenomenal range of derivative influences (embodied by Art Deco) with new indigenous expressions (reflected in "Modernism"). Within this range of new expression were merged the patterning, color and geometry of Egyptian and Aztec cultures; the probing of density and multiple images of Cubism; the dynamism and syncopated rhythms of jazz; the romance associated with ocean liners like the Normandie and the Ile de France; the glamour of the automobile and the speed of the locomotive; the daring and streamlined visions of aero-dynamics; the new realms of fantasy opened up by movies and later by animation; the intellectual and fictional stimuli of science inspired by H.G. Wells and Buck Rogers movies; the use of new industrial materials such as chrome, glass, polished bronze, and stainless steel in high design. While it

drew on virtually every form of material production, this integrated vision could be as exquisite in balance as it was vast in circumference: with only a shift in mental perspective, an architectural macrocosm could be perceived as a sculptural microcosm. Thematic harmony was at its most celebrated. And the energy of Utopian planners—Le Corbusier, I. Chanin, Buckminster Fuller, Norman Bel Geddes, and Frank Lloyd Wright—infused these new-age dreams with scope and radiance. But along with the idealism and drama of the new American style, there existed a delicate line of divine caution, for just over that line lay decadence, mediocre indulgence, and crassness.

"The 1920s was a period of bouyant optimism and dour prophesies, of Utopian aspirations butting against harsh realities."[3] As the Western hemisphere worked toward regaining itself from the agonies of World War I, America grasped at the manifestations of her new identity. Hot jazz was the musical embodiment of the time, later to undulate into the less frenetic tempos of "swing." So pervasive was that music as the spirit of the era that its rhythmic punctuations became measurably incorporated into the developing expressions of American Deco.

As America groped and shimmied through the 1920s, it became evident that this country was deriving her greatest inspirations from science and technology, embodied by the image of the *machine*. In the 1930s, technology represented the practical means and spiritual hope through which America might restore her economically and morally devastated society from the Great Depression. Technology offered superlative industrial production, efficiency in the home, fast travel, new comforts, and freedom from drudgery. Machines would give American art and architecture their own vocabulary, spelled out in the forms of stainless steel, glass, and plastics.

In the 1920s the formal machine aesthetics developed by Le Corbusier, Mies van der Rohe, the Bauhaus, the Constructivists, and De Stijl irrevocably blew apart classical architectural tradition. By the 30s, this cerebral "International Style" began to give way to a more dynamic functionalism, its organic qualities reflecting the aesthetic vitality and emotional thrust of that decade. In little more than ten years the fine arts, architecture, and the industrial and decorative arts had become synthesized ideologically, functionally and symbolically. America had grown from a society having a dilute awareness of its intrinsic creative energy to one having a manifest consciousness of design. This close-knit relationship of the arts is at the heart of the style which came to be called "Modernism."

Modernism was sustained in great part by a new contributor—the industrial designer. As industrial production increased in the 1920s, manufacturers had turned to the closest available artists for the design and promotion of their goods. Most of these artists were advertising illustrators, graphic designers, package designers, poster-artists, window-display artists, and theatrical designers, (whose talents were remarkably fitting for a period which called for dramatic solutions). The perspectives brought to this realm of work by such men as Norman Bel Geddes, Russel Wright, Henry Dreyfuss, Walter Dorwin Teague and Raymond Loewy improved the safety, utility, and appearance of products, while they also elevated standards of taste and professionalism.[4] Universal among them was a regard for the dynamic principles of "streamlining." Streamlining represented economy, efficiency, aerodynamic speed, and greater awareness of sculptural form. By cleansing surfaces of two-dimensional ornamental patterns and thereby preparing the form to move through space with the least possible resistance, streamlining came to symbolize progress and the shape of a better future to a Depression-weary society which was ready to "get things *moving* again." Not only were cars, trains, and ocean liners streamlined for aerodynamic purposes, but also furniture, appliances, typography, graphics, jewelry, and fashion—every aspect of American material life, even those not related to movement—were affected by the sleek curved style which came to be known as "Depression Modern" or "Streamlined Moderne."

As a result of all these influences, the architecture of Old Miami Beach (which was constructed primarily during the 1930s) manifested in a style that was at once theatrical, romantic, streamlined, sculptural, culturally derivative, and imbued with a sense of fantasy and animation. When the elements which had been synthesized through the Art Deco and Streamlined styles of the cosmopolitan North were transplanted from their jazz and ferment to the shores of the breezy South, the style took unto itself a tone not only particularly American but clearly, originally, and particularly Tropical.

Actually, tropical architecture had begun to have an influence on American tradition in the late nineteenth century when photographs of Robert Louis Stevenson's house in Samoa were reproduced in contemporary publications. About the same time, the "bungalow house" from India and the open Japanese house began to provoke American awareness of the tropical form. Old Miami Beach architecture incorporated this open air orientation through the consistent use of verandas for socializing and of recessed lobbies which gave structural relief to the buildings while extending the atmosphere of openness.

The hotels and apartments of Old Miami Beach share many of the compositional elements intrinsic to Moderne design: combinations of flat and curved walls; use of glass block, circular windows balanced by rectangular framing, and metal railings. But the luxurious use of ornamentation and applied detail which the tropical style indulged in gives the buildings a much more Deco orientation. "Tropical Deco" evolved out of a softer palette and had a different vision from "Big City" or "Industrial Deco," whose imagery predominantly conveyed man's control of his destiny and his domination over nature via the machine. Tropical Deco was less electric, more temperately seductive, and far less ideological. Nevertheless, it shared with the larger Art Deco style one important attitude—the *totality* and *integration* of its vision.

The community of Tropical Deco buildings on Miami Beach demonstrates an aesthetically consistent architecture, significant for the stylistic integrity of each building and for the thematic harmony by which each relates to the other and all to their environment. The sculptural and formal design of Tropical Deco hotels and apartments exhibit a dynamic exterior wholeness, animated by ornamentation based on either the geometry of their compositions or to their location on the Florida shore.

Tropical Deco buildings sit squarely on the flat Florida earth, facing into the ocean breezes. They do not ascribe to the structural aerodynamic principles of streamlined architecture. Rather, they invoke the aura of the sea more literally, with frequent nautical references like "porthole" windows, deck-like balconies, and flagstaff finials. The use of "Floridiana"—tropical motifs and colors—is another reflection of the style's conscious integration with the geography around it.

The nautical and tropical references also heighten the romance and fantasy which flavors a great deal of Tropical Deco buildings. After all, this was resort architecture, intended to lift the visitor from the gloom of the Depression, to merge his shelter with the glories of surrounding nature, and even, perhaps, to remind him of the spirituality of light and air and openness. *This was an architecture designed to evoke feelings of delight.* It was here that the movies were invited to inscribe their mark. Where else could the frivolous scenarios of Fred Astaire and Ginger Rogers be more credible than in an Old Miami Beach setting! How easily we can imagine them—or ourselves—dancing upon the rooftops of a Tropical Deco hotel in the moonlight or swaying in each others' arms beneath the palms on the beach. The unabashed romance of the Tropical Deco style was equal in every way to Fred's dreamy-eyed and immodestly declared infatuations on the silver screen.

Tropical Deco architecture in Old Miami Beach was originally planned to "advantageously combine an extremely modest construction cost with a heightened flashy, popular and modern appearance to specifically attract a new solidly middle-class group of tourists."[5] Resort buildings went up on Miami Beach at the rate of about one hundred per year in the 1930's, until World War II brought an end to construction.

By 1941, most hotels had been taken over by the military to house soldiers in training, and building materials went to the war effort. A few significant hotels of the style, such as the Delano, were built in the late '40s. It is probably that the designs of some of these had been initiated before the interruption of the war.

Many people see in the 1939 World's Fair "World of Tomorrow," the culmination of the optimistic conceptions of those futuristic designers who contributed to it; Old Miami Beach fulfilled the dreams of the decade perhaps even more completely. While the New York World's Fair set out to show that "the advances of science, the capability of technology and the wisdom of good design could shape an orderly, healthy and content society,"[6] it was not a true Utopia because it had no citizens. Old Miami Beach had few permanent citizens, but it had tourists and seasonal residents who came there to escape the economic and social woes of the country, and also to enjoy the health, glamour and romance of Florida—all of which Tropical Deco architecture reflected by maintaining aesthetic contact with the environment, climate, and people for whom it was created.

The principal architects who built Old Miami Beach were Albert Anis, L. Murray Dixon, Roy F. France, Henry Hohauser, and Anton Skislewicz. Among them, they constructed at least seventy of the most notable Deco buildings in the District. Not a great deal is known about these men. Most of them had not completed a formal architectural training. They came from Eastern Europe, from the Midwest, from New York, from Florida. Probably they considered themselves builders rather than designers; nevertheless, the inventiveness with which they used so many kinds of fantasies gave "each building its own expressive edge."[7] Furthermore, they acted as channels, open to the contiguous aesthetic forces of the time to recognize trends that were more than just economically viable. In Tropical Deco architecture they evolved a style that was vital, inviting, and perfectly suited to the time and place of its being.

1 FACADES

Perhaps nowhere have buildings less abashedly served as advertisement than in Tropical Deco architecture. Flamboyant and self-promoting in character, they capitalized on ornament and color to call attention to themselves and to animate their themes. Their original white facades were enlivened with tropical pastel accents, like the seafoam green, flamingo pink and sunny yellow racing stripes which highlighted the rhythmic nature of many structural elements. Likewise, the precise strokes of color which articulated the "eyebrows" or cantilevered sun shades.

The newly interpreted palette of the Taft Hotel inverts the dynamic of the original Tropical Deco color scheme, emphasizing both the masses and details within its crazy quilt of friezes, moldings and stripes. On the facade of the Whitelaw, wavy racing strips have been incised, creating a jazzy counterpoint to the heavier horizontal and vertical banding at center and top.

Whether symmetrical or asymmetrical, Tropical Deco buildings are strongly geometric. The frequent use of "step-backs"—the dimensional staggering of the facade plane—amplifies their sense of rhythm and lightness. The broadened step-back of the Haddon Hall molds the architectural form within and around itself, evoking an image of interlocking gears.

Fantasy and imagination were given fuller expression in the design of buildings such as the Plymouth Hall and the Warsaw Ballroom (formerly Hoffman's Cafeteria). The Streamlined Moderne image of the Plymouth, likely inspired by the trylon and perisphere, symbols of the 1939 World's Fair, calls forth the era's fascination with space, rocketry, science fiction and Buck Rogers movies.

The Warsaw Ballroom combines a collage of sculpted masses and Deco motifs with a strictly formal balance. Like the Plymouth and the very classical U.S. Post Office, it is composed with a central rotunda flanked by rectangular wings.

The Kenmore represents perhaps the cleanest and most severe facade of the Deco District. Its scarcely embellished symmetry, accentuated by the precision of its proportions, demonstrates Tropical Deco's incorporation of an International or Bauhaus style sensibility.

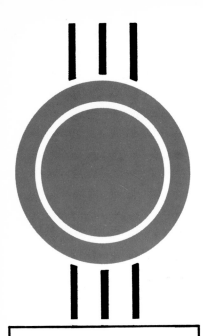

1. Taft,
   1040 Washington
   Henry Hohauser, 1936

2. Whitelaw,
   808 Collins Avenue
   Albert Anis, 1936

3. The Majestic,
   660 Ocean Drive
   Albert Anis, 1940

4. Haddon Hall,
   1500 Collins Avenue
   L. Murray Dixon, 1941
   Robert M. Schwarz, sculptor
   of cast-plaque reliefs

Fig. 1

Fig. 2

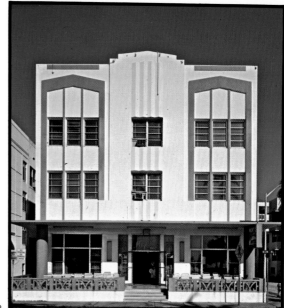

Fig. 3

Fig. 4

Many hotels are significant not only for their Deco ornamentation, but also for their symmetrical division into tripartite facades, often designed to emphasize the central plane.

Fig. 6

Fig. 5

5. Beacon Hotel,
720 Ocean Drive
Harry O. Nelson, 1936

6. Warsaw Ballroom (formerly
Hoffman's Cafeteria)
Collins Avenue and
Espagnola Way

Henry Hohauser, 1940
Robert M. Schwarz, sculptor
of plaster relief work

7. Plymouth Hotel,
336 21st Street
Anton Skislewicz, 1940

Fig. 8   The design of the Miami Beach Post Office emphasizes the classical simplicity of its geometric form.

Fig. 9

8. Miami Beach Post Office
   Washington Avenue &
   12th Street
   Cheney, 1939

9. Kenmore,
   1050 Washington
   Anton Skislewicz, 1936

2 FINIALS · PARAPETS

Having absorbed aspects of commercial showmanship from the "New York/Hollywood/Cinema" style, Tropical Deco architecture elected to publicize itself gregariously by its soaring finials, exaggerated parapets, and sculptural towers. This decorative emphasis on the tops of buildings was provoked largely by Miami Beach's inadequate zoning laws which permitted only minimum setback from the street (five feet) and allowed buildings to be built exceptionally close to one another. The ingeniously designed and varied articulations that arose above the City's low skyline served to assert the individuality of each building.

The fantastic towers of the Ritz Plaza, the Delano, and the National rise above Old Miami Beach with the quality of an architectural fiction. The Ritz Plaza is a construction of blocks topped by a cylinder, embellished with four discreet radiations. The Delano tower exalts above the skyline; its four wings seem either to have been flown forward through history from some Indian ceremonial headdress or Egyptian artifact, or foretold by some future civilization. The silver cupola of the National sits atop the hotel modestly imperial and Byzan-

tine, resting on a open Moorish base and topped by a cloud-piercing foil. On a mundane level, the tower structures of these larger hotels often served to house elevators or machinery.

The metal railings along the roofline of the Breakwater and the ship's rail contruction atop the Chatham apartments refer directly to ocean liners. The ribbed mullions on the Carlyle ascend far above the building, making the parapet an exaggerated frontispiece.

One of the Art Deco District's most sculptural ornaments is the tower-like construction of the Palmer House which progresses upward in levels and is topped by a chrome ornament. The vertical center construction of Fairmont dramatically exceeds the roofline. And the finial of the Tiffany complements that building's futuristic tone as it sits atop the hotel like some science-fictional totem.

Sculptural finials on the Royal House and the Abbey imbue their buildings with elements of fantasy and surrealism. They bring the elaborate center facade sections to a culmination and fulfill the architectural focus of the buildings.

10. Ritz Plaza,
    1701 Collins Avenue
    Delano,
    1685 Collins Avenue
    Swartburg, 1947
    National,
    1677 Collins Avenue

In the 1920s an awakened awareness of American Indian culture and the social revolutions in Latin America brought forth attention to Aztec, Maya, and Inca cultures. These developments established precedents in American design for Indian rhythms, patterns, and totems.

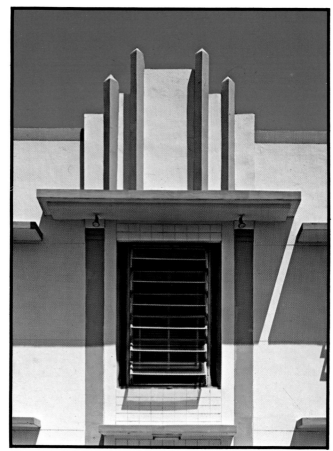

Fig. 12

Fig. 13

11. The Breakwater,
    940 Ocean Drive
    Anton Skislewicz, 1939

12. Barnett Apartment,
    1115 Euclid Ave.
    Leonard Glasser, 1949

13. *Century Hotel,
    140 Ocean Drive
    Henry Hohauser, 1939

Fig. 14

Fig

14. Fairmont,
1000 Collins
L. Murray Dixon, 1936

15. Chatham Apartments,
1676 James Avenue
Edward A. Noland, 1941

16. The Carlyle,
1250 Ocean Drive
Kichnell & Elliott, 1941

Fig. 17

Fig. 18

17. Royal House,
1201 Pennsylvania
L. Murray Dixon, 1939

18. Abbey,
300 21st Street
Albert Anis, 1940

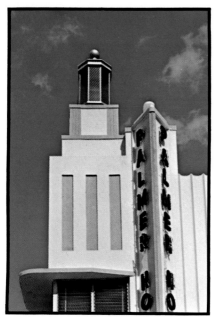

Fig. 19

Fig. 20

Fig. 21

Fig. 22

19. Palmer House,
1121 Collins Avenue
L. Murray Dixon, 1939

20. Essex,
1001 Collins Avenue
Henry Hohauser, 1938

21. Tudor,
1111 Collins Avenue
L. Murray Dixon, 1939

22. Tiffany,
801 Collins
L. Murray Dixon, 1939

3 MOLDINGS·FRIEZES

Moldings and friezes are integrated with the elements of Tropical Deco architecture into what could be imagined as a musical profusion. They draw the eye with their lyrical appeal and sustain among the architectural devices an overtone of harmony.

The frieze on Figure 23 embellishes the building with melodic lightness. The vertical sequence of leaf and rosette patterns ascends the facade toward a crescendo in the framed sunburst, from which stylized waves ripple along the parapet.

The Hotel Alden is a treasury of rhythmic designs—from the racing stripes in relief to the friezes which act as capitals of the quasi-pilasters, marching across the facade.

The moldings of the Olympic are bold and staccato. The Hotel Taft displays a series of "ribbed mullions" at each corner and in the center, where they define a cacophony of bas-relief friezes. The parapet is decorated with angular fluting, and even the doorway below has been treated with geometric relief.

When Deco Plaza was restored, its friezes and moldings were repainted to emphasize their exuberant decorativeness. Fountain and geometric patterns animate the width of the block-long apartment building.

The Evelyn frieze is a combination of vegetal, zig-zag and scallop motifs; oversized racing stripes on the Beacon are interposed with a classic Deco relief of shell patterns and Ionic gladioli. The scalloped molding of Figure 30 skirts the roofline and bottom edge of the central window.

23. Residential Apartment
Jefferson Avenue and
9th Street

24. *Alden Hotel,
2925 Indian Creek Drive
Nadel & Nordin, 1936

Fig. 25

Fig. 26

25. *Olympic,
    426 Ocean Drive
    Albert Anis, 1936

26. The Taft,
    1040 Washington Avenue
    Henry Hohauser, 1936

Fig. 27

Fig. 28

Fig. 29

Fig. 30

27. Deco Plaza
    701-45 5th Street
    T. Hunter Henderson, 1930

28. Beacon,
    720 Ocean Drive
    Harry O. Nelson, 1936

29. Evelyn Apartments
    711 16th Street

30. 1420 Collins Avenue
    E. G. Cobelli, 1923

31. Collins Plaza,
    318 20th Street
    Henry Hohauser, 1936

33

4 CUBES · PLANES

In the abstract geometry of Tropical Deco architecture one finds that the visual energy rests on the dynamic interplay of the buildings' masses and forms. Within the facades, the architectural planes are consistently interrupted by structural changes of direction, by the interjection of linear elements like the cantilevered eyebrows, and by progressive tensions and reliefs which are accomplished by the stepbacks, their periodic recessions dividing the structures into segments. This multi-dimensional aspect of Tropical Deco architecture is strongly reflective of Cubist art.

In Tropical Deco buildings, foreground and background, space and mass are rendered a rhythmic cacophony of architectural syncopations. The pure patterning of the lines of the architecture expand into a march of angles and curves.

Likewise they draw the eye inward with the application of emphatic decorative detail, as in Figure 34. The flatness of the Florida landscape lends itself to this geometric view.

As Figure 33 illustrates, the more Deco-style hotels (second and third from the right) are integrated with the more International-style hotels (on either side) by the broad bands of windows which extend across the facades like strokes in a Mondrian painting. If jazz could be manifested in architectural form, it would no doubt be in a Tropical Deco hotel.

The integration of dynamic structural elements with colorful and pronounced decorative features makes Tropical Deco buildings decidedly sculptural in effect. Many buildings have a hard-edged angularity, while the wraparound—or curving of a building around a corner—softens the look of others.

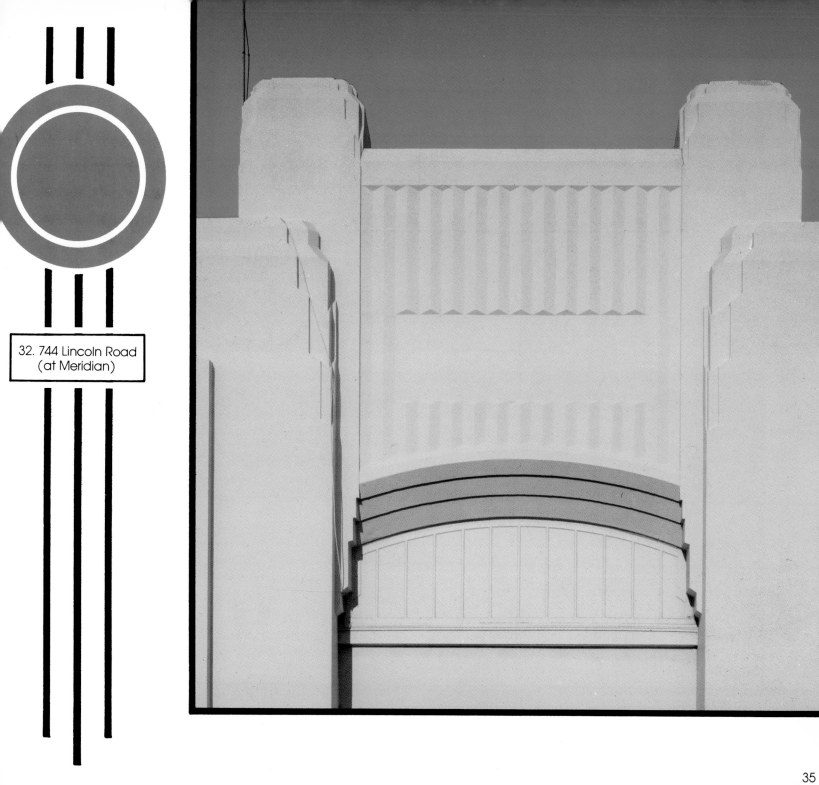

32. 744 Lincoln Road
(at Meridian)

Fig. 33

Fig. 34

33. Ocean Drive, 1985   34. Ocean Drive, 1980   35. Collins Avenue at 16th Street

Fig. 35   Viewed individually, or from several blocks away, the buildings express rhythms which are conjugated in a spectrum of levels.

Fig. 36

36. Residential Apartment

37. 1533-39 and 1521-31
Pennsylvania Ave.
Roy France, 1935

Fig. 37

The dramatic use of the "mirror image," the thrusts and recesses of two buildings identically reflecting one another, was a visual phenomenon which Tropical Deco employed.

38. Rapsodi Apartments
730 15th Street
L. Murray Dixon, 1939

5. SYMBOLS · IMAGERY

Exaggerated and profuse, the decorative imagery of Tropical Deco architecture reveals the style's romantic, naturalistic, and even flirtatious nature. Exotic birds, tropical flora, nymphs and sunrays, zig-zags, fountains, waves, and historical illustrations compose the imagery of the bas reliefs upon the facades of the buildings or etched into the glass of their windows.

The birds most commonly depicted were the flamingo, the heron, and the pelican, all of them common to South Florida in the 1930s. The attenuated lines of the flamingo and the heron lend themselves stylistically to the curvilinear quality of applied architectural decoration: they are dramatic birds, creatures of exaggerated proportions. And the pelican, a bird of greater comedy, can glide the air currents of the Gulf Stream with the same broad-winged sweep.

The symbolic use of the fountain motif represented the very process of life—rising and falling—and in more poetic terms illustrated in Tropical Deco imagery, a welling up of a natural force and the subsequent cascading downward in synchronized pattern.

Nourishing and all-pervading, the sun is depicted time and again in linear radiance, projecting its rays throughout the background of many a Tropical Deco scene. The sunbathing cult of the 1920s which popularized sun worship and heliotherapy revived an interest which had been significant in ancient Egyptian and Peruvian cultures. In these cultures, the sun was revered as a fundamental source of life, and, like the fountain motifs, its image was symbolically uplifting. And for Miami Beach, where there is hardly a day when the sun does not shine, the allusion was more literal than symbolic.

Out of the fashion of sun worship evolved naturalistic representations of nude figures in Tropical Deco decoration. Sometimes the figures were expressed in rather classical poses, as if in the act of some mythological adoration (Figure 39). At other times, like on the Royal Arms, they were illustrated in romantic settings of sensual indulgence. After all, for the northern visitor escaping the bleakness of winter and the gloom of the Depression, to see Miami Beach as the Garden of Eden was not an unlikely metaphor.

The power of nature was further invoked in the Tropical Deco use of the zig-zag. Highly derivative of Egyptian and Aztec design, the zig-zag motif was often manifested as a stylized wave or as a lightning bolt, the missile of the gods. The zig-zag also represented Art Deco's fascination with electricity and expressed the style's homage to technology.

Stylized waves, clouds and plant life (especially gladiolus patterns) amplify the organic energy of the style. They reflect the sense of perpetual growth in a climate that knows no winter.

41

39. *Surf,
    444 Ocean Drive

40. *Pelican on Miami Beach
    residence

41. Bass Museum (formerly
    Miami Beach Public Library)
    2100 Collins Avenue
    Russell Pancoast, 1939
    Gustav Bohland,
    relief sculptor

42. Bass Museum detail
    Gustav Bohland, sculptor

43. Mayfair Hotel,
    1960 Park Avenue
    Henry Hohauser, 1936

Fig. 39

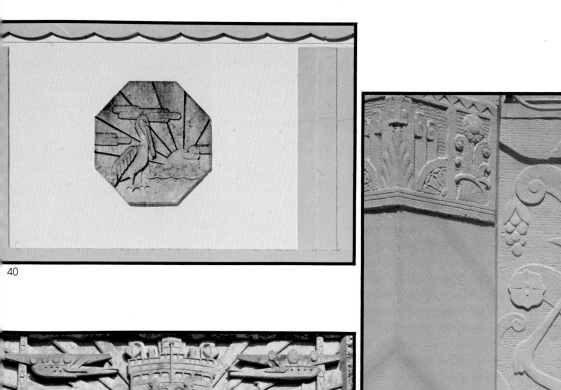

40

41

42

Fig. 43

The Bass Museum bears Tropical Deco friezes whose imagery relates the history and character of Florida. All of the pictorial representations on the Bass are represented with organic stylization and illustrate the integration of historic awareness into Tropical Deco terms.

Fig. 44

Fig. 45

The fountain motif added fluidity to the geometry of the style. Though the theme was prevalent in the Art Deco style in general, it literally found its home in the land of Ponce de Leon's "Fountain of Youth."

44. Barclay Plaza,
    1940 Park Avenue
    Krehnel & Elliott, 1935

45. Bancroft Hotel,
    1501 Collins Avenue
    Albert Anis, 1935

46. Royal Arms,
    1223 Collins Avenue
    L. Murray Dixon, 1934

6 LARGER HOTELS

Perhaps the most sculptural of all the architecture in Old Miami Beach are the larger Tropical Deco hotels north of 15th Street. Though they could not compare in height with their northern counterparts, they reflected that part of the American character of the 1930s which was enthralled with the skyscraper. Assertive in their height but never overwhelming, these structures demonstrate a clean geometry and sensuous sweeping line. In the Delano, the diagonal step-backs rise and fall across the facade like stylized Leger waves.

The New Yorker is a beautiful unit of horizontal and vertical symmetry. Above the wraparound sun shade of the ground floor, the rhythmic ascension of the hotel begins. Continuous band windows, underscored by turquoise racing stripes, bend around the curved corners of the building. Vertical turquoise bands divide the symmetry of the facade, on either side of which cast plaque friezes alternate and ascend. Vertical glass-block strips, beginning from Deco fountain bases, mark the next rising accent. The facade also includes two step-backs which add dimensional tension to its linear quality. The culmination of the New Yorker is a stepped parapet on which fluted molding compliments the curved articulations of the structure.

The St. Moritz is an asymmetrical, hard-line counterpart to the New Yorker. The beautiful spatial divisions of its facade—vertical to the left and horizontal to the right—incorporate the windows as strong design elements. And the parapet, elaborately composed with flagstaff finial, reaches high above the building like the most classical of Deco watchtowers.

The Victor is one of the few Tropical Deco hotels in which the eyebrows extend uninterrupted across the facade, giving strong horizontality. This is balanced by the soaring vertical bands, which define the southeast corner and create a sculptural form in themselves—alternate reliefs of turquoise and white that finally transcend the roofline.

In the Sands, wide bands curve around the entire building to establish its horizontal rhythm. Faceted windows achieve the curve at the building's corners, and the off-center vertical strokes on the left of the building culminate in its unusual finial-topped cupola.

The sense of pattern on the Raleigh is achieved through the use of windows. Framed by vertical panels of pink blocks at the left of center and again at the far right, the windows change their shape according to their place in the facade. They begin with staccato regularity as part of the wraparound curve at left, then diminish into tripartite units with the pink block framing. The central portion of the facade—above the keystone-framed lobby—is ornamented only by three vertical friezes at top and the subtle accent of a ship's railing. The asymmetrical geometric parapet highlights the sculptural definition of the hotel.

47. Delano,
1685 Collins Avenue
Swartburg, 1947

Fig. 48

Fig. 49

Fig. 5

Though they may not tower like New York's Empire State Building or radiate like the Chrysler Building, these larger Tropical Deco hotels were successful monuments to their own style.

Fig. 51

Fig. 52

48. St. Moritz,
    1565 Collins Avenue
    L. Murray Dixon, 1939

49. New Yorker,
    1611 Collins Avenue
    Henry Hohauser, 1940

50. Victor,
    1144 Ocean Drive
    L. Murray Dixon, 1937

51. Sands,
    1601 Collins Avenue
    Roy F. France, 1939

52. Raleigh,
    1777 Collins Avenue
    L. Murray Dixon, 1940

7 SMALLER HOTELS · APARTMENTS

Resort visitors to Old Miami Beach in the 30s were attracted by buildings that represented the flashiest and most up-to-date in popular architectural fashion. And because many of the design elements of Tropical Deco had been adapted from the Deco style prevalent in the North, the tourists were made comfortable, consciously or subconsciously, by the familiarity of the design by which they were surrounded here. Whether modest like the Commodore with its sequential bosses and wraparound, or classy like the Cardozo with its graceful streamlining, the consistency of the style pervading the resort gave it a tone of modernity.

As hotels went up along or within blocks of the Miami Beach ocean front, numerous apartment buildings emerged on the streets nearby to the west. Sharing the intimacy of scale and recurrent patterns of the average Deco hotels, these apartments expanded the utility and appeal of the style: not only did Tropical Deco represent glamour to the tourist, it also offered attractive and livable design for the "permanent" visitor.

In these apartment neighborhoods, the decorative energy became quieter in tone because the buildings were farther apart from each other and the greenery of lawn foliage softened the harshness of concrete. The casual frivolity of the applied details seems almost to tickle the white facades. And the style's consistency, block after block, heightened the feeling of community; the frequent balconies and courtyards—like the verandas of the hotels—capitalized upon the open-air, sociable tone of a Tropical Deco neighborhood.

53. Coronet Apartment,
900 Jefferson

Fig. 54

52

54. Cardozo,
1300 Ocean Drive
Henry Hohauser, 1939

55. Commodore,
1360 Collins Avenue
Henry Hohauser, 1939

56. Palmer House,
1119 Collins Avenue
L. Murray Dixon, 1939

Fig. 56

Fig. 55

Generally three stories high with classic Deco division of exterior surface, these buildings lent themselves to the social atmosphere of the Beach. No towering high-rises nor sprawling megastructures, the Deco buildings were compact and self-contained in design, and humanly scaled.

Though individually distinctive, the unity established by the cohesiveness of the style underscores a sense of "community."

Fig. 57

Fig. 59

58

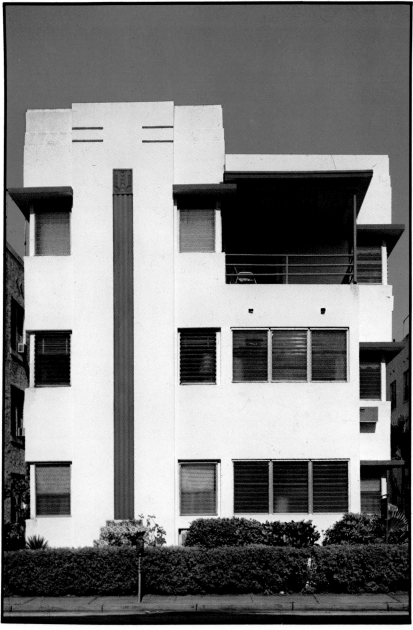

Fig. 60

57. Block of Meridian and
    15th Street

58. Kenmore,
    1050 Washington Avenue
    Anton Skislewicz, 1936

59. Residential Apartment
    Collins and 10th Street

60. Galaxy Co-op,
    852 Collins Avenue
    Henry Hohauser, 1936

Fig. 61

Fig. 63

61. Residential Apartment
    1211 Pennsylvania
    Henry Hohauser, 1939

62. Collins Park,
    2000 Park Avenue
    Henry Hohauser, 1939

63. Residential Apartment
    Jefferson Avenue
    L. Murray Dixon, 1940

8 DOORWAYS

Tropical Deco architecture often gave the doorway a conspicuous degree of theatrical attention. Embellished, articulated or ornamented, the doorway became a metaphorical as well as literal passageway from the consciously staged facade toward the drama of life within.

The doorway in Figure 64 has been developed with a kind of classical grandeur. A stepped-back door-surround, a Corinthian-Deco frieze, and metal-relief lighting fixtures are symmetrically composed around the doorway (metal door is not the original). The window articulation above and the four surrounding octagonal windows provide further emphasis of the composition.

A system of geometric patterning marks the doorway in Figure 65. The bold strokes of the sun-ray motif are balanced and expanded by the use of stripes and the alternating colors in which the entire scheme is painted.

An exuberant application of Ionic scrolls draws attention toward the doorway of Figure 66. Notice the sculptural lighting ornaments, typifying the beauty of Deco detail.

The private residences in Old Miami Beach show a significant number of highly illustrative stamped metal screen-door decorations. Stylized silhouettes of the Florida landscape, they illustrate the exotic tropical imagery with which the region was associated. Plant life is represented in virtually botanical contours, complemented by the posturing of the ever-present flamingo.

64. Residential Apartment
905 Michigan
Norden & Nadel, 1937

Fig. 65

Fig. 66

65. Dulce Apartments
700 14th Street
Henry Hohauser, 1939

66. *Residential doorway
310 78th Street

Fig. 67

Fig. 68

Fig. 69

Fig. 70

Fig. 71

67. Residential doorway
Lenox Ave. and 14th Street

68. Residential doorway
Lenox Ave. and 12th Street

69. Residential doorway
Lenox Ave. and 12th Street

70. Residential doorway
Lenox Ave. and 14th Street

71. Residential doorway
Michigan Ave. and 13th St.

72. Residential Apartment
500 14th Street
Gene E. Bayliss, 1939

A contoured pediment and fluted door-surround (mirrored in the wavy screen ornament) decorate this doorway. Conical lighting fixtures and incised bands further articulate the architectural structure in which the doorway is set.

9 WINDOWS

As an element of architectural design, windows were used to break up the flat plane of a surface, interjecting dimension while establishing a continuum of pattern and movement. Tropical Deco fenestration was affected by the linear horizontality of modern architecture and the nautical connotations of its environment. The style capitalized on window treatment to lead the eye along lines of continuous movement, while frequently referring to its nautical context.

One of the most literal of these references was the variation on the porthole window (Figures 74 and 75). Etched glass gave the architect another opportunity to incorporate the imagery of the environment or historical illustrations into window decor. (The principal glass manufacturers for Old Miami Beach were Herman Glasser and Paul Pilger; Glasser was especially renowned throughout the Beach for his etched glass designs.)

Geometric play was noticeable in the octagonal windows used in facade design. And small windows of questionable practicality were often incorporated with classic Deco motifs, shown on page 66.

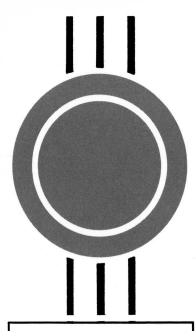

73. Tiffany,
    801 Collins
    L. Murray Dixon, 1939

74. Ambassador Hotel,
    227 Michigan Avenue
    W. F. Brown, 1925

75. Residential Apartment
    Collins Ave. and 9th Street
    McKay & Gibbs, 1947

Fig. 73

Fig. 74

Fig. 75

Keystone (oolitic limestone), tinted a sea green, is shaped around an etched-glass porthole window. Further articulations of the ocean liner theme are illustrated above.

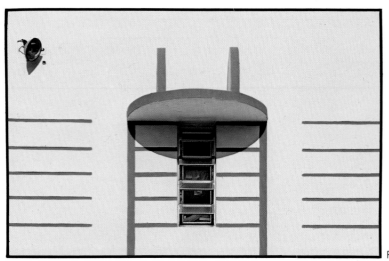

Fig. 76

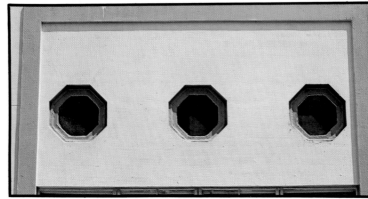

Fig. 77

Fig. 78

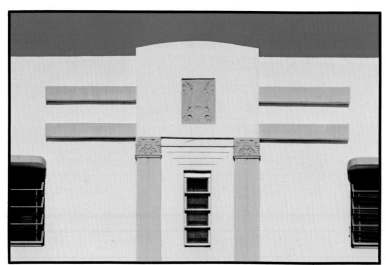

Fig. 79

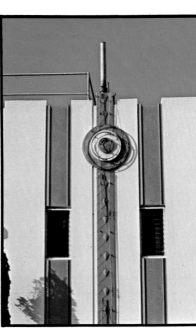

Fig. 80

76. Residential Apartment
   1559 Meridian
   Henry Hohauser

77. Park Central,
   640 Collins Avenue
   Henry Hohauser, 1937

78. Shirley Apartments
   1423 Collins Avenue
   A. Herbert Mathes, 1949

79. Residential Apartment
   1557 Meridian
   Henry Hohauser

80. Fillard,
   236 21st Street
   Henry Hohauser, 193

81. Joy Apartments
1250 Pennsylvania
L. Murray Dixon, 1940

The "faceted" treatment involved the structural placing of a series of flat windows to achieve the curving of the wraparound. This factor in Tropical Deco architecture was significant in establishing the streamlined look of the style.

10 MATERIALS

Terrazzo was a commonly used mosaic flooring made by embedding small pieces of marble or granite into concrete. In Old Miami Beach, terrazzo was frequently tinted in pastels and tropical tones, arranged in geometric patterns, and polished to an appealing gloss.

Glass block—cool and translucent, its surface industrially refined—was ideal for Tropical Deco architecture. A hallmark of modernity, glass block conducted the light of the year-round Florida sun with little transmission of heat, allowing interior surfaces to be permeated with cool light. Glass brick also offered effective sound insulation and was practical to maintain, its surface requiring no polish or paint. Furthermore, its block form added to the geometric statement of the architecture.

Glass tile, under the trade names Vitrolyte and Carrara, was used on facades and door-surrounds (Figure 84). Its use as an interior wall covering will be elaborated upon in the next chapter.

A frequent building material which related directly to the Florida geography was tinted keystone, made from the oolitic limestone indigenous to South Florida. This porous rock, sometimes patterned with fossils, absorbed the pink, cream, and sea-green tints with which it was treated for use as door-surrounds, applied columns, and balaustrades (Figure 86).

An occasional accent for Tropical Deco exteriors was the metal railing. It was often used in nautical contexts for deck-like balconies or ship-railing parapets, or decoratively as a non-functional ornament (Figure 85). Underscoring the ideals of industrial aesthetics, the stainless steel marquee, bosses, and finial of the Governor are an outstanding demonstration of an industrial material in combination with a traditional substance, here the plaster reliefs (Figure 89)

82. Mayfair Hotel,
1960 Park Avenue
Henry Hohauser, 1936

83. Davis Hotel,
1020 Washington Avenue
Henry Hohauser, 1941

. 84

Fig. 85

Fig. 86

84. Residential Apartment
   1525 Meridian
   L. Murray Dixon, 1939

85. Don Bar,
   1571-73 Pennsylvania
   Albert Anis, 1937

86. Cardozo,
   1300 Ocean Drive
   Henry Hohauser, 1939

87. Governor Hotel,
435 21st Street
Henry Hohauser, 1939

11 LETTERING

A radical transformation in typography had begun in the decades preceding the Deco period. The Russian Constructivists were the first to evolve in type an abstract design element capable of creating visual patterns that had strong emotive meanings. This was dramatically expressed in the poster art of the 20s and 30s.

Streamlining extended even to typography, and as letters dropped their serifs and ornaments, they revealed a strong geometry which could be most successfully integrated with architecture.

Many hotel doorways in Old Miami Beach were made more prominent by marquees whose streamlined lettering was unified with the total design of the building. The typeface known as "Futura," developed in the 1920s, shows the clean angularity and rounded precision apparent in much Tropical Deco signage. Likewise, the assymmetrical weight distribution of the typeface called "Broadway" is reflected in the lettering of such hotels as the Dorchester.

88. Hotel Astor,
    956 Washington Avenue
    T. Hunter Henderson, 1936
89. Dorchester Hotel
    1850 Collins Avenue
90. Governor Hotel
    435 21st Street

Fig. 88

Fig. 89

Fig. 90

These unembellished letter faces reflect the clean lines and distinct spatial divisions of the buildings they designate.

Fig. 91

Fig. 92

Fig. 93

91. Delano Apartment
    1540 Pennsylvania

92. Alexandria
    1515 Euclid

93. Royal House
    1201 Pennsylvania

12 INTERIOR DETAILS

Glass and metal lighting fixtures like those in the Victor Hotel (figures 94 and 95) were typical of the interior ornamentation in Tropical Deco resorts. The glass petals are fountain-like accents to the streamlined bases, and they illuminated with a localized and diffuse glow.

Lighting was an important consideration in Deco design schemes, and variations on its effects were widely explored. Recessed lighting produced a subtle luminescence, illuminated glass block emanated an understated iridescence, and the use of neon added a colorful excitement to the resort atmosphere. As figure 96 illustrates, neon was often recessed behind ceiling panels and various interior constructions. In the Kenmore, it amplifies the geometric design of the staircase. The expression "in the pink" was derived in the 30's when pink lighting was used in clubs and glamour spots to give skin tones a healthful and attractive glow. Other colors used in interior and exterior decorative details were red, green and yellow. Furthermore, the subliminal pulsing of the neon added a mesmerizing energy to the kinetic atmosphere of the resort.

The ceiling of the Collins Plaza demonstrates an architectural rhythm which has been carried through with detailed consistency. The three graduated tablets mirror the curves of the ceiling.

The mantel of the Cardozo (figure 100) is a Deco classic with mirrored stripes, fluting and geometric modelling. Notice also the tinted and striped terrazzo.

The Vitrolyte panels of the Astor Hotel are a dazzling arrangement of Deco color. These glass sheets were produced in panels of 4' x 4' and 4' x 8' and their thickness varied from 1/8" to 1". Here their design is interplayed with the patterning in the terrazzo and heightened by the use of black, which, while not common in Tropical Deco schemes, was a frequent color accent in the larger Art Deco style.

94. Victor Hotel
    1144 Ocean Drive

95. Victor Hotel
    1144 Ocean Drive

Fig. 94

Fig. 95

96. Kenmore
1050 Washington Avenue

97. Collins Plaza,
   318 20th Street
   Henry Hohauser, 1936

98. Davis Hotel
   1020 Washington Avenue

99. Governor Hotel
   435 21st Street

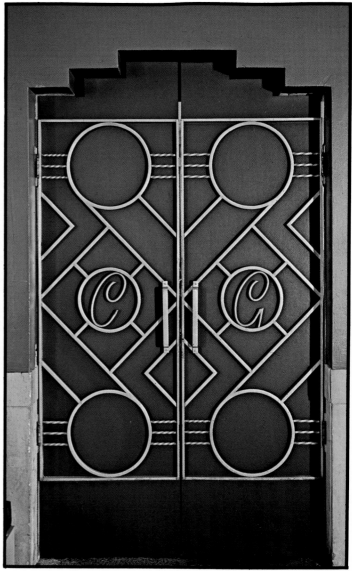

Fig. 99

A metal railing cascades down the staircase of the Davis Hotel, while a doorway in the Governor swings with a jazzy metal ornament.

100. Cardozo
1300 Ocean Drive

101. Astor Hotel
956 Washington Avenue

13 MURALS

The muralists who decorated the interiors of many Miami Beach hotels were as diverse a group of artists as were the architects who had designed these buildings. They acquired their profession through circuitous twists of circumstance as often as through predilection.

Paul Silverthorne and Wilho H. Anderson painted murals in casinos and nightclubs throughout Miami Beach, such as the Clover Club, the Latin Quarter, the Sunny Isle Casino, and the El Chico Lounge. Sadly, none of these buildings exists today. Silverthorne and Anderson began their careers in Miami Beach at the end of the 30s, after arriving there nearly penniless and eager for any kind of work. They earned a living as pastel portraitists for the tourists and color-mixers for paint companies. When a need arose for mural painters, they adapted their talents and became "creators of atmosphere." Silverthorne had been trained as a theatrical painter and had apprenticed at the New York World's Fair, working on signs and parade floats; he had no hesitation in applying his abilities to interior decoration. So abundant did he find the drama in the natural elements around him that he developed a new sense of color, becoming enamored of brilliant chartreuse and forest green, and he worked out elaborate compositions of egrets, herons, roseate spoonbills in flight, and the intertwining foliage of monstera and banana leaves.

Silverthorne and Anderson worked in the company of fellow artists like Paul Simone, Raymon Chatoff, Earl LaPan (a sculptor as well), Denman Fink, and Chuck Dodson (also a sculptor). Many of their works were exercises in color values and the dramatic effects of simplicity. "Anyone who can control his values can become a fine painter," Silverthorne expressed." Royal blue, plum, and burgundy were favored colors, and the work and color-play of the Mexican muralists Diego Rivera and Jose Orozco also influenced them.

The mural in the Colony Hotel was painted by Paul Simone around 1935. Simone projects a robust pictorial quality deeply reminiscent of the Mexican artists. The mural was painted on canvas and installed on a wall of beautiful glass tile on which three Deco racing stripes also appear.

Throughout Old Miami Beach were to be found all kinds of fountains, adding their cooling grace to the prevailing architectural style. The mural in the Flamingo Apartments is an ideal scene including both a Deco fountain and the classic Tropical Deco bird from which the building took its name.

The Depression granted few opportunities to artists, with the outstanding exception of the WPA, a federal works program through which artists were paid for their work in public buildings. The interior of the Miami Beach Post Office was designated such a project, and the wall and ceiling murals inside that building testify to the talent of muralist Charles Hardman who was supported and given a place for expression by this government program. Painted on three canvas panels, the wall mural depicts the landing of Ponce de Leon on Florida soil, and ensuing battle with the Seminole Indians. The figures are strongly modeled and idealized, the drama of the scenes captured in the Uccello-like immediacy of the narration. On the ceiling a depiction of the sun and starry sky, also painted on canvas, incorporates the ceiling fixture and its geometric grille.

A classic nineteenth-century pastoral scene has been transplanted into a tropical setting in the mural in the Plymouth Hotel by the Russian artist Raymon Chatoff. Voluptuous maidens languish in the flora while a troubadour lazily encants a ballad. Tahitian and Balinese influences are in evidence here (as they also are in Paul Simone's work) in the earthy tones and particularly in the roundness of the contoured forms.

The Cinema Theatre contains what is surely one of the finest—and richest—examples in the United States of a Deco theater interior. Originally the "French Casino," this Deco showplace was built in 1930 at a cost of around $5 million. It was a playground of Deco features: etched-glass mirrors bordered by recessed neon lighting; chrome and glass lighting fixtures; a sweeping staircase leading to a "ship's-lounge"-like balcony offering a wide view of the lobby's plaster ceiling painted in tones of mauve and taupe. A parquet dance floor was defined by blue mirrored pillars. And surrounding the dance area was a wall-length bar covered in a glittering fish-scale texture.

The theatre seated about 1,200 people. Rhythmically rounded box-seating areas flow like waves along the auditorium, from balcony down onto steps on the stage. The mural illustrated in Figure 107 is mirrored by a matching one on the facing wall.

The murals of the Tiffany Hotel amalgamate almost every conceivable Tropical Deco motif. Painted directly on the plaster walls, these murals incorporate sinewy maidens of mystical bearing with historic and geographic allusions. In Figure 108 an oceanic goddess holds out the promised Fountain of Youth above what can be assumed to be Ponce de Leon, while flamingos and sea gulls look on.

In Figure 109 an aquatic maiden answers the prayers of a native by annointing him with the gifts of the sea. And indeed those gifts to the natives of Miami Beach were bountiful.

102. Colony,
     736 Ocean Drive
     Paul Simone, muralist

103. Flamingo Plaza Hotel
1055 Meridian
Earl LaPan, muralist

104. Miami Beach Post Office
Charles Hardman, muralist

105. Plymouth Hotel
336 21st Street
Ramon Chatoff, muralist

106. Miami Beach Post Office
Charles Hardman, muralist

107. Cinema Theatre
muralist unknown

108. Tiffany Hotel
muralist unknown

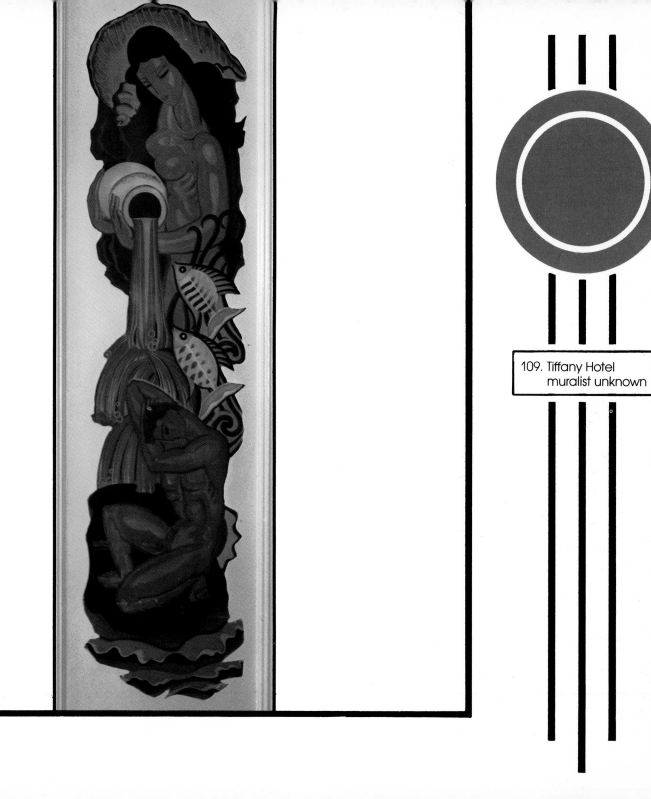

109. Tiffany Hotel
muralist unknown

NOTES BIBLIOGRAPHY

NOTES

1. Martin Battersby, **The Decorative Twenties,** (New York: Macmillan Publishing Co. Inc., 1969), p. 152.
2. Hilton Kramer, "Show at Modern Captures the Era," **The New York Times,** Arts & Leisure, Sunday, Nov. 19, 1979, Section 2.
3. Donald Bush, **The Streamlined Decade,** (New York: George Braziller, 1975), p. 21.
4. John Caplans, "Introduction," **Project Skyline** by Jewel Stern, (Akron Art Institute, 1979), p. 4.
5. Bush, **Op. Cit.,** p. 154.
6. Coplans, **Op. Cit.**
7. **Ibid.**

BIBLIOGRAPHY

Applebaum, Stanley. **The New York World's Fair 1939/1940.** New York: Dover Publications, Inc., 1977.

Battersby, Martin, **The Decorative Twenties.** New York: Macmillan Publishing Co., Inc. 1969.

Bush, Donald J. **The Streamlined Decade.** New York: George Braziller, 1975.

Capitman, Barbara Baer. "Re-discovery of Art Deco," **American Preservation 1** (August/September 1978): 30-41.

Capitman, Barbara Baer. editor. **Portfolio: The Art Deco District.** Miami Design Preservation League and the National Endowment for the Arts, 1979.

Friedman, Jeannie. "WPA Poster Projects: When Government Sponsors Art." **Print.** July-August, 1971. pp. 45-52.

Gill, Brendan. "Radio City Without Tears." **Horizon.** March, 1978. pp 89-90.

Glueck, Grace. "MOMA at 50," **Interior Design.** Vol. 1, No. 1, January, 1980. pp 262-269.

Grief, Martin. **Depression Modern, the 30's Style in America.** New York: Universe Books, 1975.

Hillier, Bevis, **The World of Art Deco,** "An Exhibition Organized by the Minneapolis Institute of Arts, July - Sept., 1971," New York: E.P. Dutton & Co., 1971.

Huxtable, Ada Louise, "Show at Modern Celebrates Its Landmarks," **The New York Times,** Arts & Leisure, Sunday, November 19, 1979. Section 2.

Kramer, Hilton. "Show at Modern Captures the Era," **The New York Times,** Arts & Leisure, Sunday, November 19, 1979. Section 2.

Lesieutre, Alain. **The Spirit and Splendour of Art Deco.** Secaucus, New Jersey: Castle Books, 1978.

Lessard, Suzannah. "The Towers of Light." **The New Yorker,** July 10, 1978. pp 32-58.

Liss, Robert. "Deco Mania," **The Miami Herald,** February 11, 1979, Tropic Magazine Section, pp 18-23.

Mumford, Lewis. **Roots of Contemporary Architecture.** New York: Reinhold Publishing Company, 1952.

Nash, Charles Edgar. **The Magic of Miami Beach.** Philadelphia: David McKay Company, 1938.

Olson, Arlene R. **A Guide to the Architecture of Miami Beach.** Miami: Dade Heritage Trust, 1978.

Silverthorne, Paul. Private conversations, 1980.

Stern, Jewel. **Project Skyline.** Akron Art Institute, 1979.

Vlack, Don. **Art Deco Architecture in New York 1920-1940.** New York: Harper and Row, 1974.